TIMEFORM'S FIFTY TO FOLLOW ON THE FLAT IN 1991

© Portway Press Limited 1991

Timeform Horses To Follow
is published and printed by Portway Press Limited, Halifax, West Yorkshire HX1 1XE.
It is supplied to the purchaser for his personal use
and on the understanding that its contents are not disclosed.
Every care is taken in the compilation of Timeform Horses To Follow,
but no responsibility is accepted by the publishers
for errors or omissions or their consequences.

ISBN 0 900599 53 7

ARZANNI
AZZAAM (USA)
CABOCHON
CASTORET
CHESNUT TREE (USA)
CHILIBOY
COLLINS AVENUE (USA)
DARTREY (IRE) ∎
DESERT SUN
DOMICKSKY ∎
ENVIRONMENT FRIEND
EVASIVE PRINCE (USA) ∎
GILT PREFERENCE
GOLDEN CAP (USA)
GREEN LANE (USA)
HABAAYIB
IMPERFECT CIRCLE (USA) ∎
ISLAND UNIVERSE (USA)
JAWANI (IRE)
LA BAMBA ∎
LILIAN BAYLISS (IRE)
LIVE ACTION
MARJU (IRE) ∎
MATADOR (USA)
MUKADDAMAH (USA)
MY BED TIME
NO DECISION
OPERA HOUSE ∎
PALATIAL STYLE
PERSIAN HOUSE
PLAYFUL POET
POLISH KING (USA)
REGENT'S FOLLY (IRE)
REPIQUE (USA)
RIVER GOD (USA) ∎
RUN FOR NICK (FR) ∎
SALMINO (IRE)
SARCITA
SERIOUS HURRY ∎
SHAHI (USA)
SHEIKH ALBADOU
SPRING TO THE TOP
STAGECRAFT
STRAW BERET (USA)
SWIFT SWORD
TAKADDUM (USA) ∎
THE CAN CAN MAN
TIDEMARK (USA) ∎
WAKASHAN
WALIM (USA)

For those who prefer a smaller selection ∎

ARZANNI

4 gr.c. Darshaan
Astara (Nishapour (FR))

The Aga Khan might have stopped racing his horses in Britain following the Aliysa affair but his home-bred Arzanni will continue to run here for the same stable, having been sold to Mr David Thompson shortly after victory under top weight of 9-7 in the £14,750 Sun Life of Canada Garrowby Stakes at York last September. That victory in a limited handicap was Arzanni's third in a season which had begun with defeat in a claimer. Obviously he'd improved tremendously by the time he ran at York. Arzanni continued on the upgrade. On his next appearance he found the moderate early pace against him, and finished unplaced, in the Festival Handicap over a mile and a half at Ascot; but stepped up to two miles in the listed George Stubbs Stakes at Newmarket in November he put up a fine staying performance. Held up, travelling much more strongly and comfortably than in his races against useful middle-distance handicappers, he moved forward from three furlongs out, was ridden into the lead over a furlong out, and stayed on splendidly to win by three lengths from the Cesarewitch winner Trainglot, another much improved colt who started favourite ahead of Arzanni.

As with so many of the French Derby winner Darshaan's stock, staying is clearly Arzanni's game. He should pay to follow at a mile and three quarters or more. On his latest form he should be able to hold his own in pattern company, but he is still on an official rating which will let him into some of the big long-distance handicaps, and his trainer may elect to go for one or more of them in the first half of the season. A big, lengthy, quite attractive colt, Arzanni has raced only on a sound surface so far, and has done all his winning on good to firm. **L. M. Cumani**

**Arzanni
beats Trainglot**

AZZAAM (USA) ❙ 4 ro.c. Chief's Crown (USA)
Princess Oola (USA) (Al Hattab (USA))

Followers of Timeform's weekly Horses To Follow phone line will already be familiar with the lightly-raced and progressive Azzaam. He was recommended on 'the line' last October after gaining a comfortable success in a competitive Newmarket handicap and justified our faith in him when spreadeagling a twenty-three-strong field in the William Hill November Handicap. At Doncaster he put up a very useful performance under 9-8 in beating Army of Stars by three and a half lengths, and provided all remains well with him—muscle trouble followed by the dry summer delayed his preparation last year—he should make his mark in pattern company. A tall, close-coupled colt with a sharp action, Azzaam has won on good to firm ground but goes particularly well on soft. He stays a mile and a half well.
J. L. Dunlop

CABOCHON ❙ 4 b.g. Jalmood (USA)
Lightning Legacy (USA) (Super Concorde (USA))

Cabochon improved out of all recognition towards the end of 1990, winning three of his last five starts, and there's every reason to believe he'll pick up where he left off. He was untried at two and spent the first half of his three-year-old season racing over middle distances, largely on top-of-the-ground, with the result that he was unplaced in his first five starts. Given a chance to tackle a longer trip on easier ground, he took off and won two handicaps at Nottingham and another at Newcastle in the autumn. His first success came in workmanlike style off a mark of 58 at Nottingham and it's a measure of his improvement that he won comfortably off a mark 16 lb higher at Newcastle on his final start. He was still full of running at the end of a strongly-run race over two miles on soft ground at Newcastle, and could keep ahead of the handicapper for a while yet.

Cabochon's dam Lightning Legacy was never tried beyond a mile and remained a maiden after ten starts, but she's well bred, being out of the smart Leave It To Me, and she's proving a success at stud. Her first foal Black Monday developed into a useful · middle-distance handicapper, and Cabochon is her second. The third, Cache (by Bustino), is an unraced three-year-old with Luca Cumani. **D. Morley**

CASTORET ❙ 5 b.g. Jalmood (USA)
Blaskette (Blast)

Castoret is now in his sixth year yet has had only eight races in his career—he was unraced at two then had an interrupted campaign at three—and in essence is relatively unexposed. We did get some idea of his potential in a handicap at Lingfield in the closing weeks of the 1990 season. Faced with the stiffest test of stamina he's so far encountered—a mile and a quarter on soft ground—he easily defied top weight of 10-0, forging clear inside the last furlong and being value for even more than his six-length margin. On the all-weather there over a week later, he found conditions altogether different and hadn't the pace to mount a challenge.

Considering his pedigree, it's surprising Castoret hasn't yet been tried over further than a mile and a quarter. His sire is generally regarded as an influence for stamina, and his dam was a tough and genuine middle-distance handicapper who, incidentally, enjoyed her best season as a five-year-old, winning four races including the Falmouth Handicap and Daily Mirror Handicap. To our mind Castoret will improve when stepped up in distance; and considering he's still well handicapped on the form he showed when successful, it will be surprising, not to say disappointing, if he doesn't manage to add to his score this season. With regards to his ground requirements, it's probably significant that Castoret was raced solely on an easy surface in 1990 and ran moderately on the only occasion he encountered very firm ground. **J. W. Hills**

CHESNUT TREE (USA) | 3 b.f. Shadeed (USA) Expansive (Exbury)

The 1985 Two Thousand Guineas winner Shadeed and the 1979 Ribblesdale Stakes winner Expansive had just three races between them as two-year-olds. Their daughter, Chesnut Tree, ran just the once. Starting at 20/1, she finished fifth of twenty, catching the eye with some good late work, in the maiden event won by Campestral over seven furlongs at Newmarket in November. She was leggy and unfurnished as a youngster, and her Newmarket run was given her probably for the purpose of letting her see a racecourse before being put away for the winter. Like her dam, she is going to stay and mature late. Obviously, we don't know enough about her to predict how good a racehorse Chesnut Tree is going to be, but she's bred more than well enough, looks a fair sort, and performed with sufficient promise in her one run to suggest she's bound to win a maiden event at least. Incidentally, she hasn't changed stables since last season: rather, her trainer William Hastings-Bass has since been elevated to the peerage. **Lord Huntingdon**

CHILIBOY | 4 gr.c. Precocious Chili Girl (Skymaster)

Those who followed the sprinting scene during the late-'eighties should have no problem remembering John Dunlop's Chilibang. A powerful grey, occasionally wayward and best in blinkers, he climaxed a rather chequered racing career by winning the King's Stand Stakes at 16/1 and is now resident at the National Stud. Judged on what he's shown so far Chilibang's half-brother Chiliboy seems unlikely to make his presence felt against the best sprinters, but he's still a horse to enthuse over. A chipped knee-bone restricted Chiliboy to just a couple of

**King's Stand Stakes (1988)—
a win for Chiliboy's half-brother Chilibang,
from Governor General and Ever Sharp**

outings as a juvenile, and after his first eight attempts as a three-year-old all he had to show for his efforts was a narrow win in a Pontefract maiden event. However, dropped down to five furlongs for the first time in a handicap at Redcar in October he put up a smashing performance, showing fine speed from the start to beat Le Chic and fourteen others decisively. Chiliboy was turned out again at Doncaster a couple of weeks later only to run below form, eased right down once his chance had gone, behind another of our Fifty To Follow Playful Poet. The testing conditions seemed all against him that day, and the stocky Chiliboy, who's probably best in blinkers nowadays, can be relied on to leave that form well behind back on a fast surface. He's still an unexposed horse at the minimum trip, and we're confident he'll make up into a useful performer in the coming season. **J. L. Dunlop**

COLLINS AVENUE (USA)

**3 b.c. Linkage (USA)
Trolling (USA) (Sir Gaylord)**

Collins Avenue's debut in division two of the Dunkirk Maiden Stakes for two-year-olds over six furlongs at Doncaster in November had promise written all over it. 10/1 from 6/1, and green in the preliminaries, he took time to realise what was required from the stalls and soon got behind. He was still halfway down the field with two furlongs to run, where his rider had to check to avoid some scrimmaging, but once switched to the centre of the track he stayed on most strongly, making ground hand-over-fist to finish two lengths second to the more experienced Reshift. He drew six lengths clear of the remaining sixteen runners and seems sure to win races with this behind him.

Collins Avenue's finishing run at Doncaster leads us to believe he'll stay a mile, and on breeding he should get further. His sire Linkage was high class at up to nine and a half furlongs, finishing second in the Preakness Stakes, while his dam Trolling was a minor winner at up to nine furlongs. Trolling is a half-sister to Raise Your Skirts, who won nine of her fourteen races at distances of five to nine furlongs, and is the dam of the high-class sprinter Big Shuffle. Collins Avenue looked unfurnished at Doncaster, and showed a markedly round action once racing. He is unlikely to prove high class himself, but he should have little difficulty winning a maiden and it wouldn't surprise us to see him go on and more than recoup the 15,000 dollars he cost as a yearling. **B. W. Hills**

DARTREY (IRE) **| 3 b.f. Darshaan**
Secala (USA) (Secretariat (USA))

Like several others in this booklet Dartrey made only one appearance in 1990, and such was the style of her victory that we've no hesitation in nominating her as a filly to follow. The race in question was the Oh So Sharp Stakes over seven furlongs at Newmarket on Cambridgeshire day. Dartrey faced seven opponents—five of them winners—and despite looking in need of the race she beat them in most impressive fashion. The early pace wasn't particularly strong, and with three furlongs to run most of the field were in contention. Dartrey produced a fine turn of speed to burst into the lead soon after, however, and on meeting the rising ground she galloped on really strongly, as Diamond City came clear in second, to win by three lengths with ears pricked. Dartrey is quoted in the ante-post market for the One Thousand Guineas at around 20/1, and the pace she showed at Newmarket suggests she could well make her presence felt in that race. However, if she lives up to her pedigree she will come into her own over middle distances. Her sire the Prix du Jockey-Club winner Darshaan looks like becoming a marked influence for stamina—his five individual winners of six pattern races in Europe during 1990 all won at either ten or twelve furlongs—and her dam has already produced Sir Simon (by Sir Ivor), who showed useful form to win the Ulster Harp Derby over eleven and a half furlongs. Whatever her optimum trip turns out to be it's highly likely that Dartrey has a good deal of improvement in her, and unless we're very much mistaken she'll have a say in some of the best races for fillies in 1991. **M. R. Stoute**

| Dartrey
is most impressive

DESERT SUN

3 b.c. Green Desert (USA)
Solar (Hotfoot)

Green Desert made a most promising start to his career as a stallion, just holding off Bering for the title of leading first-season sire judged on prize money won in Great Britain and Ireland. And whilst, unlike Bering, he cannot yet claim a pattern winner amongst his progeny, we'll be surprised if that's still the case at the end of 1991, for as well as Volksraad, the impressive winner of a Newmarket maiden in November, he will be represented by Desert Sun. Making his only racecourse appearance as a juvenile, Desert Sun, a strong colt with a long, round action, ran out a most impressive winner of a Doncaster maiden over seven furlongs in October; soon travelling strongly in the lead, he quickened readily when shaken up at the three-pole and ran on really well until eased by Steve Cauthen inside the final fifty yards. On paper that race would appear less than competitive, but the manner of his victory, and the enthusiasm with which it was achieved, earmarks Desert Sun as a most interesting prospect. It's probable that he'll stay a mile—his dam, Solar, showed useful form at up to a mile and a quarter at three—and he looks likely to have a good season at around that distance in 1991. **H. R. A. Cecil**

Doncaster—
no danger to Desert Sun

DOMICKSKY

3 b.c. Dominion
Mumruffin (Mummy's Pet)

Brighton isn't a course that immediately springs to mind when looking for prospective horses to follow, but one of the first to be pencilled in for this year's 'fifty' was the twice-raced Domicksky, who won a seven-furlong maiden on the track in September. He won by only half a length but in no way does that reflect his superiority. Domicksky travelled much the best of the field for most of the race and looked likely to win in good style when sent smoothly to the front two furlongs out. However, he didn't find as much as seemed likely and needed to be driven out to hold the renewed challenge of Fast Run. Domicksky had shaped promisingly in a six-furlong Yarmouth maiden two months earlier, showing very good speed to lead for five furlongs then fading as lack of condition told. From what we've seen of him so far Domicksky looks to have plenty of pace. He comes from a fast family. His dam Mumruffin, useful and very speedy, is a half-sister to Claudius, who was placed in the July Stakes and Prix Robert Papin in 1972. Domicksky is the fourth foal of Mumruffin, and is a half-brother to the fair winning sprinter Grand Prix (by Formidable). Domicksky has already shown he acts on firm ground. He's one to follow in handicaps. **M. J. Ryan**

ENVIRONMENT FRIEND

3 gr.c. Cozzene (USA)
Water Wood (USA) (Tom Rolfe)

Following the winners of the divisions of the Westley Maiden Stakes as three-year-olds was largely disappointing between 1986 and 1990: only one of the ten horses concerned showed a level-stake profit. The ten weren't exactly seen out frequently on the racecourse either, mustering between them just thirty-one runs in Britain for five wins at odds between 15/8 on and 100/30. Good reason you might think to avoid following the race's winners in 1990, Environment Friend or Sapieha. Well, yes; but . . .

The Westley Maiden, run over seven furlongs at the Cambridgeshire meeting, has a long-established reputation as one of the very best maidens in which to spot future stars. Over the five years preceding 1990 Old Vic, Indian Skimmer, Doyoun, Batshoof, Magical Wonder, Assatis, Charmer, Blue Stag, Two Timing and Kefaah were among many future good-class performers to appear in the race. Environment Friend has better prospects than most in the latest runnings of joining that list. He had one race before the Westley, showing very promisingly at Sandown in mid-September; he'd probably have won with previous experience. In the Westley Maiden, he was joint-favourite in a field of eighteen which included runners from many of the top stables. On looks at least, his appeared the stronger division (Environment Friend is a close-coupled, useful-looking colt, by the way). He looked useful in performance as well, running on resolutely in the closing stages to lead fifty yards out and win with something in hand by half a length from Fly To The Moon with Barkerville and the subsequent winner Sharifabad close up. The Horris Hill was under consideration for Environment Friend's next outing (he was also still a Dewhurst entry at that stage) but in the end the colt was put away for the season, and the race was won by stable-companion Sapieha.

It's impossible to say at this stage how good Environment Friend might be, but he is a horse of some potential and we should have a much clearer idea of him after he's run in one of the spring trials. It is also difficult to judge what his optimum trip will be. He ran at Newmarket as if he'll prove even more effective at a mile but that might have been the result of his inexperience. His pedigree is difficult to read and one can't say with confidence at present how far beyond a mile, if at all, he'll stay. Whatever his fate we're more than hopeful that Environment Friend will enhance the record of the Westley Maiden for attracting future stars. **J. R. Fanshawe**

EVASIVE
PRINCE (USA) | 3 b.c. Secreto (USA)
Overstate (USA) (Speak John)

There weren't many winners on the turf over the straight course at Lingfield last season who raced away from the hugely favoured stand rail. There were even fewer who never came off the bridle. One who did both was Evasive Prince, who on his second outing enjoyed such superiority that his rider Swinburn was able to treat all thirteen opponents with the utmost contempt. Having shaped with plenty of promise in a maiden at Yarmouth, Evasive Prince started odds on to go one better at Lingfield in a similar event. There was never any stage that defeat looked possible and he crossed the line hard held, a length and a half ahead of his closest pursuer Oka Flow. Just how much he had in reserve is anybody's guess. Both of Evasive Prince's races as a two-year-old were over seven furlongs; a mile and a quarter should be well within his capabilities at three. An unfurnished Secreto half-brother to many winners, notably champion Canadian colt Overskate (by Nodouble) who was successful at up to a mile and a half, Evasive Prince would be the proverbial 'certainty' if asked to turn out for an early-season handicap. He appeals strongly as one to follow, and will almost certainly leave the description 'handicapper' well behind before the season is very old. Significantly, he's one of five Stoute-trained nominations for the 1991 Chrysler Triple Crown Challenge in America. **M. R. Stoute**

GILT
PREFERENCE | 4 b.g. Pitskelly
Mandolin (Manado)

Gilt Preference is another included for middle-distance handicaps. He's had little chance to show what he can do so far, but the signs are promising. His first run in a handicap, which followed three outings necessary to qualify for a mark, brought a comfortable win from seventeen opponents over a mile and a half at Leicester in October. His second, over the same trip at Newmarket, ended in defeat, but Gilt Preference ran well all the same in going down by a length and a half to subsequent winner Oshawa in a field of twelve. Gilt Preference was having his first outing for Martin Pipe at Newmarket, having been bought out of Michael Jarvis' stable for 31,000 guineas at the Newmarket Autumn Sales. He had his attentions turned to hurdling in December, starting at odds on for a juvenile event at Haydock, but could finish only ninth after setting a good pace to three out. Waiting tactics have been used on Gilt Preference on the Flat, and they may bring about improvement over hurdles, but it's as a Flat-racer that he most interests us. He's still lightly raced and his handicap mark looks on the low side.

Gilt Preference, a tall, unfurnished gelding with scope, is the only foal of the modest ten-furlong winner Mandolin. His sire Pitskelly won the Free Handicap and the Jersey Stakes in 1973, plus the following year's Bunbury Cup, when trained by Jarvis. So far Gilt Preference has put up his best efforts on a sound surface. **M. C. Pipe**

GOLDEN CAP (USA)
3 ch.f. Hagley (USA)
Mrs Hat (Sharpen Up)

Golden Cap may not be one of the more obvious choices as a horse to follow, nevertheless the manner in which she won her only race at two should ensure she keeps one step ahead of the handicapper, initially at least. Co-favourite for an eight-runner five-furlong maiden event at Wolverhampton in September, Golden Cap disputed the lead throughout but showed distinct signs of greenness and was tenderly handled from start to finish. With her jockey still sitting very quietly, she narrowly got the verdict over Negeen, a winner of a similar contest next time out, with the third horse three lengths away. The form of the race doesn't amount to much, but we can see her learning a lot from her kind introduction and rising to greater heights.

Sprinting will no doubt be Golden Cap's forte. Her sire Hagley was a speedy two-year-old in America, although his best performance came when winning the Withers Stakes over a mile at three. Easily his best runner to date has been the high-class sprinter Committed. The dam Mrs Hat, successful at around six furlongs in the States and granddaughter of the One Thousand Guineas winner Glad Rags, also produced the 1988 Irish two-year-old six-furlong winner Plume Poppy and a winner in Italy from previous matings with Hagley. **P. F. I. Cole**

GREEN LANE (USA)
3 ch.c. Greinton
Memory Lane (USA) (Never Bend)

We had this colt down as a sure-fire winner of a mile nursery last autumn but he was retired for the season before he had the chance to oblige. Actually, Green Lane should have been the comfortable winner of such an event at Warwick in early-October on his final outing. He finished fastest of all in sixth of twenty-two, having quickened well when he finally got some room over a furlong out after being poorly placed much of the way, involved in scrimmaging at least twice. The riding tactics were hard to understand—to hold him up was to invite trouble given the size of the field. Waiting tactics had also been employed in his two previous (unplaced) runs, whereas before that he'd made all in maiden company over a mile at Chepstow.

Green Lane can take up in 1991 where he left off in 1990, in handicap company, that is, and should develop into a fair animal over middle distances. A step up from a mile will suit him extremely well. His dam may strike a chord with some readers. She was in Balding's stable in the 'seventies and showed useful form, winning the 8.5f Princess Elizabeth Stakes at Epsom first time out as a three-year-old; she's a sister to Mill Reef, and is the dam of several winners, including the useful middle-distance filly Fields of Spring (by The Minstrel). The sire Greinton is a Green Dancer horse. He started his racing career in France but found fame in the States, through, amongst other things, winning the Hollywood Gold Cup Handicap and the Santa Anita Handicap, both Grade 1 races over a mile and a quarter. Green Lane has had only five races, but already it is clear he acts well on firmish ground. **I. A. Balding**

HABAAYIB | 3 ch.c. Blushing Groom (FR)
Awaasif (CAN) (Snow Knight)

In recent years the seven-furlong EBF Yattendon Maiden Stakes at Newbury in August has been chosen to mark the introduction of several horses who have gone on to make a name for themselves, most notably Minster Son, Unfuwain and Nashwan. In all probability the latest running of the race unearthed another future star or two; the first four finished clear, with the third and fourth, Arokat and Jahafil, going on to fill second place in the Laurent-Perrier Champagne Stakes and Royal Lodge William Hill Stakes respectively. However, it was another newcomer, the runner-up Habaayib, whom we liked especially. A leggy colt with scope, Habaayib looked just in need of the race. He made progress from three furlongs out and ran on strongly in the closing stages, just failing to peg back Balaat, who had the experience of a previous outing. Habaayib is certainly bred to be a good horse; he's a full brother to Snow Bride, awarded the Oaks on the disqualification of Aliysa, out of the Yorkshire Oaks winner and Arc third Awaasif. A mile and a quarter-plus will prove right up his street in 1991—there are plenty of races to be won with him. **M. R. Stoute**

IMPERFECT CIRCLE (USA) | 3 b.f. Riverman (USA)
Aviance (Northfields (USA))

What appeals to us about Imperfect Circle as a horse to follow is not so much that she was able, in just three starts in her first

**Imperfect Circle
wins over six furlongs at Ayr**

season, to win a listed event over six furlongs at Ayr and run second in the Tattersalls Cheveley Park Stakes over six furlongs at Newmarket, as that she was able to attain such a high level of form at a distance one would normally regard as too sharp to bring out the best in a filly by Riverman out of a mare by Northfields. The excellent speed she possesses is going to stand her in good stead in high-class fillies' events at a mile to a mile and a quarter, and we wouldn't be in the least surprised if she were to prove every bit as smart as her half-sister Chimes of Freedom, who ran second in the Cheveley Park Stakes in 1989. Chimes of Freedom did not come to herself in time to contest the first fillies' classic, and it may be worth noting (equally, it may not) that Imperfect Circle, a tall, attractive filly, was not asked to do much until the autumn; nevertheless, we cannot help thinking that she represents extraordinary good value each-way at her pre-season quote of 33/1 for the One Thousand Guineas.
R. Charlton

ISLAND
UNIVERSE (USA)

**3 b.c. Lyphard (USA)
Carefully Hidden (USA) (Caro)**

Island Universe is an intriguing Guineas contender and we await his reappearance in one of the classic trials—the Craven at Newmarket or the Greenham at Newbury seem the most likely alternatives—with great interest. His taking on some of the more exposed members of his generation should be informative. Luca Cumani is one of the modern school of trainers who, so far as his

Island
Universe

more promising youngsters are concerned, regards two-year-old racing as primarily a preparation for the future. He ran Island Universe just the once, against seven other newcomers in the Duke of Edinburgh Stakes over six furlongs on good to firm going at Ascot in October. Looking back on the race now, it's difficult to say for sure what the form's worth, but Island Universe could scarcely have impressed more in winning. A rangy colt, apparently short of peak fitness and in need of racing experience, a weak favourite at 3/1 too, he moved up on the outside to take command in a matter of strides around two furlongs from home, and came right away. We made his margin over the runner-up Arylh (herself a clear winner next time) nearer ten lengths than the official seven.

Island Universe may well prove best at up to a mile, as did his sister Ensconse who won the Goffs Irish One Thousand Guineas in 1989. Interestingly, Ensconse had just a couple of races at two years, both over six furlongs, winning a maiden at Nottingham and the Blue Seal at Ascot. Before the Irish Guineas she also won the fillies' trial at Newmarket, the Nell Gwyn Stakes, and finished fourth on that course when favourite for the Guineas. Their dam Carefully Hidden, a seven-furlong winner in the States, is a half-sister to the dams of several high-class horses including Cumani's Media Starguest. Whatever Island Universe's fate in the Guineas, he should go on to win good races. **L. M. Cumani**

JAWANI (IRE) | 3 b.c. Last Tycoon
Fabled Lady (Bold Lad (IRE))

One of our more speculative horses to follow is Jawani. Last season he had two runs within a fortnight in mid-summer maidens at Salisbury and Sandown, beating only three horses home, then had three months off before finishing seventh of thirteen, never placed to challenge and beaten about nine lengths, in a back-end Leicester maiden over a mile. Our reasons for including him can be summed up in three words—fitness, physique, stamina. Jawani hasn't looked fully fit on any of his racecourse appearances so he can be expected to do better on that count alone. His physique—he's a big, rather leggy colt, a horse with scope—is that of one much more likely to make a three-year-old than a two-year-old. Most importantly he showed improvement when tried at a mile at Leicester and will improve further over a mile and a quarter. Although his sire Last Tycoon is best remembered as a top-class European sprinter who also won the Breeders' Cup Mile, his pedigree contains more stamina than his record might suggest. Jawani's dam Fabled Lady showed modest ability over a variety of distances up to a mile and a half in Ireland; she comes from the family of Princess Pati and Seymour Hicks. Jawani will start the season towards the bottom of the handicap and, hopefully, pick up a couple of bread-and-butter races as he progresses. He has raced only on top-of-the-ground. **Dr J. Scargill**

LA BAMBA | 5 br.g. Laxton
Ribamba (Ribocco)

Patience has paid dividends with La Bamba and should continue to do so in 1991. He failed to make the racecourse as a two-year-old and again at three, and apparently his owner was once advised by a vet to give up hope of ever seeing him on the track. However, La Bamba stood up really well to quite vigorous campaigning as a four-year-old, and the way he progressed in the last two months of the season marks him as a horse who could prove a moneyspinner. La Bamba broke his duck in a handicap at Redcar in September and looked unlucky not to follow up in a big field at Warwick nine days later, finishing with a flourish having virtually walked out of the stalls. The two performances which really caught the eye, though, were those he put up on his final starts at Yarmouth and Doncaster. At Yarmouth La Bamba was one of the easiest winners of a handicap we've seen in a long while, cruising through to lead on the bridle over a furlong out and drawing clear effortlessly to beat a big field by five lengths hard held. Things weren't quite so easy under a penalty at Doncaster, but La Bamba gave those who made him 9/4-favourite in a field of twenty-two few anxious moments, leading from the distance and needing only to be nudged along to win with plenty in hand.

La Bamba is a leggy gelding by the useful sprint handicapper Laxton out of a mare who's produced another notable late-developer, namely the good-class mile to mile-and-a-quarter performer Commodore Blake. Commodore Blake recorded a couple of disappointing efforts during his career, finishing last when fancied for the Cambridgeshire two years running, but there's no suggestion La Bamba is in any way unreliable. On the contrary, he seems most consistent, and with further improvement on the cards he looks sure to win more races over seven furlongs or a mile. His record to date suggests he acts on firm and dead going. **G. A. Pritchard-Gordon**

LILIAN
BAYLISS (IRE) | 3 b.f. Sadler's Wells (USA)
Godzilla (Gyr (USA))

A promising second in a twenty-six-runner maiden race at Newbury in August followed by a comfortable five-length success in a seven-furlong minor event at Chester in October is a short summary of Lilian Bayliss' first season. To add more detail, she did particularly well at Newbury, being the only one of the first eleven home to race on the stand side and staying on strongly to go down by a length and a half to Zonda, having been green to post and through the first half of the race. At Chester, she came in for plenty of support and landed the odds in impressive style. Quickening nicely on the outside, she led over a furlong out and was pushed clear inside the last to see off six rivals with the minimum of fuss.

There are plenty of winners in Lilian Bayliss' close family. By Sadler's Wells out of Godzilla, successful several times at up to about a mile in Italy at two, she is a sister to the very useful French colt Ernani (who, surprisingly, seems best short of a mile), a close relation of the high-class miler Phydilla (by Lyphard) and a half-sister to, amongst others, the Irish Derby runner-up Observation Post (by Shirley Heights). A lengthy, rather sparely-made filly with a roundish action, Lilian Bayliss has so far raced only on an easy surface. She's certain to improve again from Chester and to stay at least a mile as a three-year-old. We'll be surprised if she fails to add to her tally. **M. R. Stoute**

LIVE
ACTION | 4 b.c. Alzao (USA)
Brig o'Doon (Shantung)

Live Action ended his first season in such excellent heart that it's impossible not to be extremely bullish about the prospects for his second. Sore shins, chiefly, kept him off the track until June 1990 and although he won a maiden at Sandown the following month, leading on the line having been pushed along in the early stages, it was only when he got soft ground in the autumn that Live Action really came into his own. A mile-and-a-quarter handicap at Doncaster saw him annihilate eight opponents, making most and galloping on with great enthusiasm;

then he was made an odds-on shot in a smallish field for a nine-furlong minor event at Newcastle nine days later, and won with all the anticipated ease and more. Connections must have bemoaned the lack of days (five) left to run in the 1990 turf season. A good-bodied half-brother to Young Generation (by Balidar), Live Action can resume winning ways in handicaps as a four-year-old but might well turn out to be a bit better than that. He stays one and a quarter miles well (his only attempt at one and a half was on top-of-the-ground) and looks extremely well suited by soft going. **L. M. Cumani**

MARJU (IRE) | **3 br.c. Last Tycoon**
Flame of Tara (Artaius (USA))

With the whole of Britain well and truly in the grip of winter at the time of writing, the 1991 turf season seems a long way off. Yet before long the pieces in the classic jigsaw puzzle will once again begin to fall into place. One thing that must have been puzzling everyone since he made his debut at York last September is where Salsabil's half-brother Marju will fit in. It will be disappointing if he doesn't have a major role to play. On his only appearance so far he ran rings round ten opponents in the seven-furlong Avondale New Zealand Graduation Stakes on firmish going at York. The opposition was of no more than average maiden standard, so the form represented by his six (nearer eight) lengths and three win from Road To The Isle and Salic Dance falls well short of the level of that attained by the winners of the top two-year-old races; but the promise of the

**| Marju
and Willie Carson**

performance, particularly by one so well bred, was the stuff of which mid-winter dreams are made.

A slight set-back kept Marju out of his intended debut race in June, and when he did appear, over a distance slightly longer than his trainer would have preferred, he looked as though the run would do him good. A sturdy, lengthy colt, he did the job with the minimum of fuss, pulling double over the others from early in the straight and drawing right away once he'd gone ahead around a furlong out. Whatever else, he clearly possesses a fine turn of acceleration. After this Marju became one of the favourites for the Two Thousand Guineas, his backers no doubt aware that not even his half-sister had done better on her first run. And backers rightly recognize that Marju is bred well enough to win a Guineas. His sire Last Tycoon was the best horse in Europe in 1986 over five furlongs and went on to win the Breeders' Cup Mile in the States; his dam Flame of Tara was a high-class mare, winner of the Coronation Stakes and Pretty Polly Stakes. The question of Marju's stamina will become much more pressing a matter after the Guineas, for he's virtually certain to get the mile. In our opinion he'll stay at least a mile and a quarter, and he must have more than an outside chance of getting a mile and a half at Epsom. **J. L. Dunlop**

MATADOR (USA) **❙ 4 ch.c. Nureyev (USA)
Allicance (USA) (Alleged (USA))**

Long-standing subscribers will know of our liking for lightly-raced, progressive, middle-distance stayers; and Matador is a horse that fits the bill perfectly. Unraced at two, Matador won a four-runner maiden at Kempton in mid-summer on his second start but didn't begin to show his full potential until the last couple of months of the turf season. He put up fair efforts to be placed in mile-and-a-half handicaps at Windsor and Kempton, though just found wanting for pace, then put up his best performance on his final start in a Newbury handicap over an extended mile and five furlongs. Close to the pace from the off, he led early in the straight and galloped on stoutly to the line; the further he went the more readily he looked like winning. He beat two other progressive types, Noble Endeavour and Grey Power three lengths and one and a half with the remainder of the ten-runner field well strung out.

Matador is almost certainly capable of further improvement, particularly over a mile and three quarters or more. His style of running suggests he'll be well suited by a distance of ground and there is nothing in his pedigree to dissuade us from that judgement. He did run poorly over a mile and three quarters at Goodwood on the third of his six starts but the firm ground rather than the trip was probably responsible for that. The ground was good at Newbury, the easiest Matador has raced on. The leggy Matador is likely to be aimed at handicaps on the better tracks, generally competitive events where any success should be at rewarding odds. **R. Charlton**

MUKADDAMAH (USA) | 3 b.c. Storm Bird (CAN)
Tash (USA) (Never Bend)

Mukaddamah? Which one's that, you may well ask. These Arabic names can be confusing, and Mukaddamah is not to be confused with the three other leading two-year-olds of 1990 who directly precede him in the form-book index, Mujaazif, Mujadil and Mujtahid, nor with the older colt that follows directly after, Mukddaam. The Lambourn-based Mukaddamah finished second to Peter Davies in the one-mile Racing Post Trophy at Doncaster in October, for all except the final stride of the last three furlongs looking certain to add to his two victories, from two previous starts, one of them in another pattern race, the seven-furlong Lanson Champagne Vintage Stakes at Goodwood. Mukaddamah put up a smart performance in defeat and, all things considered, has a brighter future than some of his more-heavily campaigned contemporaries. A rangy, attractive colt who should thrive physically, he has a particularly effective turn of foot—which settled his first two races swiftly and took him from last to first in a matter of strides at Doncaster—and he should be a force to be reckoned with at up to a mile or a mile and a quarter this season.

Mukaddamah, bought for 375,000 dollars as a yearling at the Keeneland July Selected Sale, is the fifth winner out of his dam Tash. The dam won over six furlongs. None of her first three foals has won beyond seven but her three-year-old of 1990, Queen of Women (by Sharpen Up), was successful over an extended mile and a quarter in the French Provinces late in the year, and there is plenty of stamina on that side of the family. Tash's half-sisters include the Oaks-placed Arkadina, dam of the Irish St Leger winner Dark Lomond, while among her half-brothers are the King George third Gregorian and the good stayer Blood Royal; her grandam Natasha is a half-sister to the Leger winner Black Tarquin. **P. T. Walwyn**

MY BED TIME

3 b.f. Blakeney
Noddy Time (Gratitude)

All things considered, My Bed Time did more than enough on her only start at two to suggest that she won't be long in adding her name to the already long list of winners produced by her dam Noddy Time. The sprinter Grey Desire (by Habat) and a mile-and-a-quarter performer The Dunce (by High Hat) have so far proved the best of them, whilst another, Father Time (by Longleat), showed improved form as he was stepped up in distance in the latest jumping season, winning over three miles at Wetherby in February. Noddy Time herself stayed a mile well and is from the same family as High Line. The fact that My Bed Time is by the renowned influence for stamina Blakeney and that she's a late foal (June 5th) makes her effort in a six-furlong maiden race at York in October all the more meritorious. A small, workmanlike filly, she looked a bit backward and green but really got the hang of things in the final two furlongs and ran on to such effect that she finished fourth of the ten runners, a little more than five lengths behind the winner Roger de Berksted, a winner next time out, too, as was the runner-up Corn Futures. A mile and a quarter, at least, will show My Bed Time in a much better light as a three-year-old. At that distance and upwards she should do well in handicap company. **M. H. Tompkins**

NO DECISION

4 br.g. King of Spain
Really Fine VII (pedigree unknown)

The Jockey Club handicappers now allocate separate all-weather and turf ratings, the turf rating being 11 lb less than the all-weather one in the case of northern handicapper No Decision. We don't believe No Decision is one of those horses apparently transformed simply by the switch to all-weather racing. The alternative, and much preferred, explanation for his two improved efforts, winning a claimer on the first of them, at Southwell at the end of his three-year-old season is that those were his only races to date over a mile. From what we'd seen of No Decision previously, there wasn't much doubt that he'd be suited by a step up to that distance. We therefore begin the 1991 turf season with the rather anomalous situation whereby No Decision has his best performances at a mile but will be officially rated on his efforts at two furlongs less. He should be able to take full advantage. His merit as a horse to follow doesn't lie solely in the disparity between those handicap ratings. A heavy-topped gelding with scope, unraced as a two-year-old, No Decision looks the sort to train on really well. Of his nine races at three years, in which, incidentally, he was often slowly away, only five were on turf, and we feel it would be a trifle hasty to hold hard-and-fast opinions on his ground requirements. **M. W. Easterby**

Colorspin, shown beating Fleur Royale in the 1986 Irish Oaks,
is the dam of Opera House
and a half-sister to the dam of Stagecraft,
Bella Colora

OPERA HOUSE

3 b.c. Sadler's Wells
Colorspin (High Top)

'Mark down Opera House as a horse to follow: he's not a
physically imposing animal, a leggy, close-coupled individual
who looked a bit green in the paddock but fit and well; he
spreadeagled his field in highly impressive style and I haven't the
slightest doubt he's a good prospect; he's not bred to shine at
two years but the speed he showed to win this suggests he's
already considerably above average; he was always going well,
led on the bridle three from home, looked a little green when
chased along just for a stride or two out but eventually
strode clear to win without being put under any sort of pressure;
he needs rating with a large 'P' and a thumping good note.'

Thus our representative at Leicester on October 16th reported
the racecourse debut of Opera House, a son of Sadler's Wells
and the Irish Oaks winner Colorspin, in the eleven-runner EBF
Reference Point Maiden Stakes over seven furlongs for which he
started 11/10 on and won ten lengths. Little needs adding except
to say he's bred to stay a mile and a half and has the potential to
win anything. **M. R. Stoute**

PALATIAL STYLE

4 b.g. Kampala
Stylish Princess (Prince Tenderfoot (USA))

With the favourite at 9/2 and only two (including, incidentally, Azzaam) of the fourteen runners at odds longer than 16/1, the betting is one way to illustrate the competitive nature of the 'Finest Hour' Handicap, the last race on the card at Doncaster on St Leger day. But the name of the race turned out to be a prophetic one for Palatial Style—he hacked up. For much of the straight Palatial Style and John Lowe were towards the rails with nowhere to go, but when the gap finally did arrive a furlong out, Palatial Style quickened in fine style to put three lengths between him and his nearest pursuers Western Ocean and Dashing Senor. Palatial Style had progressive form over shorter distances earlier in the season, staying on well in other quite valuable handicaps at York on his two previous outings and winning at Carlisle in April and Ripon in June. The mile and a quarter trip at Doncaster, however, seemed to suit him ideally. When returned to the course for the November Handicap, he appeared to find a mile and a half in testing conditions overtaxing his stamina, though there must be a possibility that the soft ground also played its part in his below-form eighth of twenty-four amongst those strung out like washing behind Azzaam; regular racing on top-of-the-ground was no bar to Palatial Style's good progress in the summer. The official handicapper, by the way, seems to have taken the view that he'd given Palatial Style too much to do at the weights in the November Handicap and has dropped him to a mark only 1 lb higher than that off which he recorded that sparkling success in the 'Finest Hour'. We predict that there'll be a few more moments to savour from this gelding in 1991. **M. Avison**

PERSIAN HOUSE

4 ch.g. Persian Bold
Sarissa (Reform)

A second season and a distance of ground should see Persian House realise his potential. A big, good-topped gelding who didn't see the racecourse at two, Persian House ran six times last season, doing best on the last of those races, a handicap over Redcar's extended thirteen furlongs in late-October. It was the furthest that Persian House was asked to race but the moderate early pace didn't bring his stamina into full play; at the post Persian House had stayed on from mid-division to be second of the fifteen runners. This isn't a horse with a turn of foot, but maturity, forceful riding tactics and a longer trip should combine to see him pay his way in modest handicap company in the North. Persian House has won over hurdles during the winter and it shouldn't be long before he opens his account on the flat. He seems to act on both good to firm and dead ground but has yet to race on anything more extreme.

Persian House is half-brother to several winners, including the smart middle-distance colt Sabre Dance (by Dance In Time), who put up his best performances as a four-year-old, and the Irish mile-and-a-half to two-mile-one-furlong winner Inquest (by Caerleon), who registered his first success at the same age. **J. M. Jefferson**

PLAYFUL POET

4 ch.g. The Noble Player (USA)
Phamond (Pharly (FR))

A progressive and fairly lightly-raced sprint handicapper who seems to go particularly well with plenty of give in the ground—that's as good a way as any of summing up Playful Poet at the end of his second season, and, granted suitable conditions, he should continue to prosper as a four-year-old. Playful Poet wasn't seen out after April at two, by which time he'd already got off the mark in a Folkestone maiden event. He then had another lengthy lay-off after making a promising reappearance in the latest season—during which he left Kim Brassey's yard—but he returned in the autumn and proved himself better than ever, finishing second in well-contested handicaps won by The Shanahan Bay at York and Sea Devil at Newcastle. On the strength of those performances he was the subject of some sizeable bets for the George Farndon Handicap at Doncaster. He justified the support with authority, showing good speed throughout against the favoured stand rail and being driven out to beat Glencroft by a length, the pair clear of a big field. Playful Poet, a deep-girthed, strong-quartered gelding, starts the season on a very fair mark despite being upped 6 lb for his Doncaster win. More importantly, perhaps, Playful Poet gives the impression he may well have further improvement in him. That being so, his astute trainer seems bound to place him to advantage over five and six furlongs in the coming season. **M. H. Easterby**

POLISH KING (USA)

3 gr.c. Danzig (USA)
Sintra (USA) (Drone)

Late-season two-year-old races regularly throw up impressive winners but seldom one so impressive as Polish King. It is impossible to say how much Polish King had in hand when defeating Caithness Cloud by two lengths in the Soham House Stakes at Newmarket; apart from adjusting his reins briefly a furlong and a half from home, Swinburn let the colt complete his progress up the Rowley Mile hard on the bridle. Almost certainly Polish King had little to do—only four of his ten opponents had run before—but what he had to do, he couldn't have accomplished in better style. Recent winners of the Soham House Stakes include Belmez, Kahyasi and Dancing Brave, and

**▌ Polish King
has any amount in hand**

although these are very early days yet to be talking of Polish King in the same breath as any of that illustrious trio, it is difficult to escape the conclusion that he's a colt with genuine classic aspirations whose claims to be included in our 'fifty' must be regarded as outstanding.

Polish King is prominent in the betting for both the Two Thousand Guineas and the Derby but seems to us to be much more of a Guineas candidate. That success at Newmarket came in the style of one with no shortage of pace, and his American pedigree doesn't convincingly suggest one likely to stay a mile and a half. Polish King's dam Sintra is a seven- and eight-and-a-half-furlong graded stakes winner out of the minor stakes winner (at up to seven furlongs) Misty Plum. Polish King is Sintra's second foal, and fetched 450,000 dollars at Keeneland, nothing out of the ordinary for a yearling by Danzig. Danzig has sired top-class performers over a mile and a half—the Belmont winner Danzig Connection came in his second crop—but is more often associated with horses best at shorter distances, almost exclusively so in Europe where he's been represented by such as Polonia, Polish Precedent, Green Desert, Shaadi, Danehill and now Dayjur. **M. R. Stoute**

REGENT'S FOLLY (IRE)

**▌ 3 ch.f. Touching Wood (USA)
Regent's Fawn (CAN)
(Vice Regent (CAN))**

Regent's Folly cost only 10,500 guineas as a yearling at Newmarket's November Sales, and her connections look to have acquired a bargain. Not only has she won two of her three races, one quite a valuable York nursery, but she looks certain to go on and add to her tally in handicaps at three. The margin of both her victories, at Leicester in a maiden auction in September and at York the following month,was a neck, and she impressed with her attitude on each occasion, staying on resolutely to lead a furlong out and rallying well. Regent's Folly's pedigree reads as one whose future lies over middle distances and that's just how we see her developing. A good-bodied daughter of the St Leger winner Touching Wood, she's the second foal of the staying maiden Regent's Fawn, and a half-sister to Fallow Deer (by Jalmood), successful over a mile and a quarter in 1990. Regent's Fawn is a sister to the top-class Canadian middle-distance filly Bounding Away and a close relation to the high-class mile-and-a-quarter winner Ascot Knight. Regent's Folly acts on good to firm ground and has yet to race on a soft surface. **W. Jarvis**

REPIQUE (USA) | 3 ch.f. Sharpen Up
Repetitious (Northfields (USA))

Repique will come on considerably for her race at Newmarket at the back-end. She looked particularly green when asked to quicken running into the Dip, but on meeting the rising ground picked up really well without being hard ridden and, making up a couple of lengths on Shihama in the closing stages, would have got up in another few yards. The two pulled four lengths clear, and the time for the race was over a second faster than that recorded by the winner of the second division of the same maiden. A 210,000-guinea yearling, Repique comes from a good family. Two of her half-brothers, Sarhoob (by Alydar) and Sifting Gold (by Slew O'Gold), were pattern-race winners in France, the latter from Starstreak in the Prix La Force at Longchamp last May. Their dam Repetitous, a sister to Nanticious, won the Stewards' Cup and was later a stakes-placed winner in North America. Repique will stay a mile, and shouldn't have any difficulty winning a maiden before going on to better things. What you can be sure of is that her trainer will place her to best advantage. **L. M. Cumani**

RIVER GOD (USA) | 4 b.c. Val de l'Orne (FR)
Princess Morvi (USA) (Graustark)

Henry Cecil has two good staying prospects in River God and Great Marquess. We've chosen the former as a horse to follow: he beat the subsequent Jockey Club Cup winner by two places and more than three lengths on merit when third to Snurge in the St Leger on his final outing of last season and will probably keep in front of him in 1991. River God was more forward than his stable-companion early on as a three-year-old, but probably wasn't ready for the task when allowed to take his chance in an admittedly open Derby and finished down the field behind Quest For Fame. That was only his third run, his first outside maiden company. In four subsequent races River God tasted defeat in only the St Leger, winning over two miles in the Queen's Vase at Royal Ascot and over a mile and three quarters in other listed events at Newmarket and Goodwood (the Tia Maria March Stakes). River God won by a long way at Royal Ascot but his four-and-three-quarter-length third to Snurge was his best effort so far and represents a level of form as yet unattained by the vast majority of his would-be opponents in this season's distance events. While River God doesn't possess the middle-

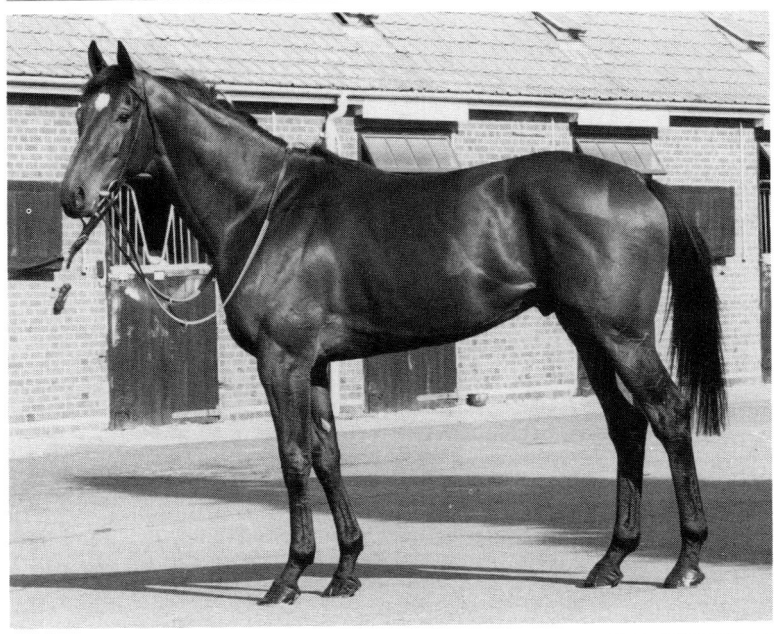

**The good-looking
River God**

distance pace of the likes of Snurge he has the ability to sustain a powerful gallop which will make him a formidable contender in the Cup races.

Well made, with plenty of scope, River God is a full brother, by the 1975 French Derby winner, to the Japan Cup winner Pay The Butler. His dam, who won at up to eleven furlongs in France, is from a good staying family; the grandam Silana won the thirteen-furlong Prix de Royallieu and is a half-sister to Barado who won the three-mile Prix Gladiateur. River God has yet to encounter a soft surface; he clearly handles firm ground well. **H. R. A. Cecil**

RUN FOR
NICK (FR)
**3 b.g. Nikos
Run For Juliet (USA) (Model Fool)**

Visibility deteriorating to just a few yards made race-reading impossible for most of the nine-race programme at Folkestone on the last day of the 1990 turf season. It was already decidedly moderate by the time of the first race, but we saw enough in that to conclude that in Run For Nick there's a horse who'll prove rewarding to follow in handicaps. That Folkestone run was Run For Nick's third in quick succession in maiden races. On each occasion he was allowed plenty of time to find his stride before putting in his best work at the finish without being given a hard race, emerging eighth of twenty-one at Pontefract, tenth of seventeen at Yarmouth and, most eye-catchingly, third of seventeen to Samurai Gold at Folkestone. There's little doubt that he will prove capable of better and his patient campaigning thus far should ensure that he has plenty of room to progress up the handicap. Run For Nick should also be a fitter horse than most when the turf season opens here at Doncaster on March 21st as he's been campaigned in Cagnes-sur-Mer. The official handicapper seems not to take much notice of results at Cagnes-sur-Mer and Run For Nick appears to have done well there on his one run at the time of writing, finishing second of eighteen over a mile on the first day of the meeting.

That performance suggests that Run For Nick almost certainly stays a mile. Whether he'll get further isn't readily apparent from a study of his pedigree. He's from the second crop of Nikos, a high-class performer at seven furlongs and a mile in France, while Run For Nick's dam and her previous offspring all raced on the Continent as well. Run For Juliet was placed at a mile and a mile and a quarter but failed to win a race. Several of her progeny have, including a couple by Brinkmanship who were successful at up to eleven furlongs. **A. A. Scott**

SALMINO (IRE) | 3 b.c. Salmon Leap (USA)
Amina (Brigadier Gerard)

Salmino provided us last year with another example of the type of horse we are fond of quoting who went from nothing (or apparently nothing) to quite useful in hardly any time at all. First time out saw him seventh of fourteen in the maiden race won running away by Steam Ahead at Hamilton in late-August; such none-too-bright specimens as Mr Reiner, Glenairlie and Sheslikethewind were among those in front of him. Before September was through he had won two races; at Edinburgh dead-heating with Bombe Surprise in a maiden event he would have lost in another stride; and at Redcar bouncing out of the stalls and making every yard of the running under top weight of 9-7 in a sixteen-runner nursery, Mr Reiner 18 lb and fourteen places behind him.

Salmino's dam wasn't up to much, and she hasn't bred all that much; but she won at a mile and a quarter and is a sister to Princess Eboli, who won the Cheshire and Lancashire Oaks. His sire, Salmon Leap, ran a good race in the Arc. So one would expect Salmino to get at least a mile and a quarter. Also to go on. Two-year-olds improving as rapidly as Salmino undoubtedly were last autumn usually carry through to their second season. **Mrs G. R. Reveley**

SARCITA | 3 b.f. Primo Dominie
Zinzi (Song)

Sarcita's place here is based on an impressive display last time out. Then it can scarcely be based on anything else, seeing that the rest of her form—one placed effort from four starts—is not worth a light. Folkestone in November was the scene of Sarcita's final appearance, and, in a field of seventeen for a six-furlong nursery, Sarcita, an eye-catching seventh, apprentice-ridden at 7-4, in a nursery at Newmarket the previous month, was backed to 4/1 co-favourite. There was no chance of her catching anyone's eye here. Visibility was very poor. A T.V. camera picked her up, briefly, in front around halfway, and when the field finally emerged from the gloom, some two furlongs or so later, it was a procession, Sarcita leading it in clear by five lengths and the same. Merryhill Maid, who finished third, had defeated twenty rivals running away by five lengths in a claiming nursery at Newmarket on her previous appearance.

This was the first time Sarcita had run over six furlongs, and the first time she had encountered a soft surface. But one doesn't have to belong to Mensa to appreciate that, whatever the reason (she had, incidentally, been trained elsewhere on her first three appearances) Sarcita was a much better filly at Folkestone than she had shown herself to be, or had the chance to show herself to be, at any time previously. For our part, we wouldn't be in the least bit concerned about her being brought back to the minimum distance. True, she would find herself up against opponents, generally speaking, faster than those which she had led such a merry dance at Folkestone, but on what we saw of her that day we shouldn't think there's the slightest doubt that speed is her forte. And if she can do it once, she can do it again. With a little bit of luck, twice over. **D. R. C. Elsworth**

SERIOUS HURRY

3 ch.c. Forzando
Lady Bequick (Sharpen Up)

One modest effort on dead ground aside, Serious Hurry did nothing but improve as a two-year-old and there's every reason for believing he'll continue to progress at three. He raced five times in all, showing little when not fully wound up on his debut but then running really well to finish second in maidens at Catterick and Wolverhampton in the autumn, at Wolverhampton battling on in splendid fashion and just going down to Negeen. Following his disappointing run, he came back with an easy six-length win on the all-weather at Lingfield in November. Serious Hurry has raced only at five furlongs and we've no doubt he'll prove best at sprint distances. In appearance he's every inch a sprinter—strong and heavy-topped—and he has a sprinter's pedigree, being a half-brother by Forzando to two sprint winners, notably the useful Joytotheworld (by Young Generation). His dam Lady Bequick raced only as a two-year-old when successful at five furlongs. Serious Hurry has shown he acts well on a sound surface. He's just the sort to have on one's side in handicap company. **Sir Mark Prescott**

SHAHI (USA) | 3 ch.c. Shahrastani (USA)
First Kiss (Kris)

Shahrastani was never likely to make a sire of precocious two-year-olds and it wasn't greatly surprising that it took until the end of October for him to sire his first two-year-old winner in Britain and Ireland, Blue Daisy over a mile at Leopardstown. That his son Shahi could show as much promise as he did on his racecourse bow augurs well for 1991 when he should develop into a more than useful colt over middle distances.

Shahi made his debut early in October in a one-mile maiden at Newmarket where he was third favourite in a field of fourteen. The most striking point about his performance was how he overcame evident inexperience—he was constantly whinnying in the preliminaries and started slowly in the race—to run third, beaten half a length and two and a half lengths, behind Hilti's Hut, who had run once previously, and Another Bob. At the finish Shahi was staying on well under a typically-sympathetic Cauthen ride. The experience will benefit Shahi tremendously and races are sure to come his way when tried over a mile and a half. His sire, the 1986 Derby winner, was, of course, well suited by the latter trip while his dam First Kiss won over a mile and a quarter. First Kiss was out of Primatie, a daughter of Vaguely Noble and the top-class middle-distance filly Pistol Packer. Workmanlike in appearance, Shahi moved well to post at Newmarket, and, all in all, has much to recommend him. **H. R. A. Cecil**

SHEIKH ALBADOU | 3 b.c. Green Desert (USA)
Sanctuary (Welsh Pageant)

We didn't see much of Sheikh Albadou—he raced only once, in a six-furlong Newmarket maiden in October—but from what we did see there was most certainly a lot to like. Very weak in the betting, he finished eighth of the eleven runners behind Chimayo, beaten around seven lengths, but shaped considerably better than his position suggests. Soon recovering after a slow start, he travelled strongly up with the leaders for much of the way and wasn't knocked about in the slightest when beginning to falter in the last furlong. A strong, good-bodied colt who looked backward and green in the preliminaries, he's sure to benefit from this considerate introduction. Sheikh Albadou is the fourth foal of Sanctuary, an unraced half-sister to Little Wolf and Smuggler, and is a half-brother to two winners at up to seven furlongs by Known Fact. He seems certain to win races and continue Green Desert's good start at stud. **A. A. Scott**

SPRING TO THE TOP | 4 b.c. Thatching
Queen of The Brush (Averof)

The lightly-raced Spring To The Top is one to keep on the right side, judged on his last-gasp victory in a seven-furlong handicap at Sandown on his final start as a three-year-old. His winning margin over Anna Karietta, a head, understates his superiority, as a troubled run on the turn forced Spring To The Top to be switched then come from well off the pace in a sixteen-runner field. He was made favourite that day following a particularly luckless effort in a similar contest at Kempton. The way in which Spring To The Top cut down his rivals at Sandown suggests that a mile will suit him better. Evidence to support this view can be found, if not on the sire's side of the pedigree, then certainly on the dam's. Spring To The Top is a close relation of the Irish filly Bristle (by Thatch) who showed fairly useful form as a two-year-old in 1985, when she won over an extended mile, and was later placed three times at a mile and a half. The dam Queen of The Brush won over a mile and a half in Ireland and amongst her several other winning progeny is the useful middle-distance stayer Princess Genista (by Ile de Bourbon) and the Sallust middle-distance performer Imperial Brush.

The rather leggy Spring To The Top is a moderate walker and shows a round action in his faster paces. He has raced only on good to firm and good ground to date and it was good at Sandown when he registered what we're sure will prove the first of several successes in handicaps. **J. W. Payne**

STAGECRAFT I 4 b.c. Sadler's Wells (USA)
Bella Colora (Bellypha)

'The Coldstream Guards Association Cup' ran some risk of being looked back on as a pretentious title for a three-year-old maiden race at York in October, but in fact the event attracted as good and interesting a field as could be anticipated for the time of year, the first two places going to two very well-bred animals in Stagecraft and Wasnah. Stagecraft, a strong, lengthy colt, is the first foal of the 1985 One Thousand Guineas third Bella Colora. He'd had his problems and was making only the third appearance of his career at York, where he put up a fairly useful performance in holding on by half a length from the filly. Much better followed from Stagecraft in the James Seymour Stakes, a listed race at Newmarket three weeks later for which he was the picture of well-being in the paddock. Only the progressive Philharmonia of his six opponents made a race of it, and she posed much less a threat than the three-quarter-length verdict suggests, for the winner, having been waited with, had taken a three-length lead running through the final quarter-mile before Swinburn stopped riding him with a hundred yards to go.

Clearly, season's end was untimely for Stagecraft's connections, but he looks the sort who will go on to win them a good prize as a four-year-old at a mile and a quarter or a mile and a half. Stagecraft has yet to tackle the latter distance, but a step up from a mile and a quarter promises to suit him well—in contrast to the experience of his dam who was put back to a mile and nine furlongs, winning the Prix de l'Opera at Longchamp, after finishing fifth to Oh So Sharp in the Oaks. Fast

**Stagecraft (left)
is much too good for Philharmonia**

ground suited Bella Colora ideally. Her son has so far raced on only good or dead. **M. R. Stoute**

STRAW BERET (USA)

**3 ch.f. Chief's Crown (USA)
Mostly Sunny (CAN) (Sunny)**

Give Straw Beret another chance. That was the conclusion after she'd finished only third in a twenty-two-runner maiden race at Doncaster having made a highly promising debut in a minor event at Newbury. It's reasonable to assume that the very soft ground was probably against her at Doncaster—she'd been withdrawn on account of similar conditions at Haydock two weeks earlier—and physically she looks the type to do much better at three than two. A rangy filly with plenty of scope, she put up the most noteworthy performance of the day behind Fragrant Hill at Newbury. Having been left with plenty to do in a slowly-run affair, she quickened in really good style approaching the final furlong and gained rapidly on the leaders close home without being at all hard ridden. Straw Beret and the well-touted newcomer Desert Sun dominated the betting at Doncaster, but after tracking the winner for much of the way Straw Beret couldn't quicken in the final two furlongs and was beaten six lengths. A Chief's Crown half-sister to several winners, notably the Kentucky Derby winner Sunny's Halo (by Halo), Straw Beret will stay a mile and a quarter. There's every chance that she's better than she's shown so far, and she should make her mark in minor contests and handicaps in the coming months. **J. H. M. Gosden**

SWIFT SWORD | 3 gr.g. Sayf El Arab (USA)
Lydiate (Tower Walk)

Dual-purpose trainer Mary Reveley has gone from strength to strength since being granted a full licence in 1981. She's on her way to recording her highest-ever number of winners over the jumps in the latest season and her 1990 Flat season was most successful, with fifteen winners and nearly £100,000 in prize money. The handicapper Mellottie was the main contributor but the two-year-old Swift Sword also more than paid his way, winning three times, and we think he'll do so again this year. His first two wins were gained in auction events at Beverley in June, over five and seven and a half furlongs, and he went on to win a York nursery in September over a mile. His prospects of victory at York looked slim three furlongs out as he found himself behind a wall of horses; however, he burst through to lead a furlong and a half out and ran on very strongly to win by a length from On Strike, the pair three lengths clear. Little attention need be paid to the fact that Swift Sword failed to make the frame in nurseries on his final two starts. On the second occasion he was impeded by a loose horse and never able to get on terms. Swift Sword will stay a mile and a quarter. He's a half-brother to the winning stayer Snowy River (by Sagaro) and Impecuniosity (by Free State), a winner over eleven furlongs; and the dam Lydiate won over a mile and a quarter. Swift Sword is a leggy, quite good-topped gelding, a moderate mover in his slower paces. He acts on firm ground and the only time he raced on a soft surface was on his final start. **Mrs G. R. Reveley**

TAKADDUM (USA) | 3 ch.c. Riverman (USA)–Lyphard's Holme (USA) (Lyphard (USA))

Inasmuch as he is a choicely-bred inmate of a leading stable and won a late-season maiden at Folkestone on the last of his three appearances as a two-year-old, Takaddum may be said to be the carbon copy of Safawan, one of our 1989 nominations. If his career continues along the path trodden by that particular horse, we shan't complain. Chances are it won't, though, at least not all the way. For Safawan progressed way beyond our expectation as he won three good handicaps in a row from four starts as a three-year-old and trained on into a smart miler. Had

**Riverman,
sire of three of this year's 'fifty'**

he not done well, obviously we would not be quoting him here, but his success serves to illustrate what can be found if one knows where to look. The salient point about Safawan is that he was allowed to find his feet in modest company and not thrown into the deep end until he was man enough to survive there. Given the same sensible management, we don't see how Takaddum, a compact, robust individual, can fail to pay his way as a three-year-old. We said he is choicely bred, and is most certainly that—by Riverman, one of the world's leading sires, out of a Lyphard mare who won twice at around nine furlongs in France and whose Ribot dam was successful in the Italian Oaks. **P. T. Walwyn**

THE CAN CAN MAN
**4 b.c. Daring March
Dawn Ditty (Song)**

It may seem less than sensible, a bit like shutting the proverbial stable door, to nominate The Can Can Man as a horse to follow in 1991 after he won four races in 1990. So, why have we done so? Well, in the first place he hasn't had all that much racing for a big, rangy individual built to withstand a lot of work; in the second place the general level of his form in the second half of last season, when the ground was on the soft side, doesn't read so good as his form on fast going earlier in the year, despite his success on softish ground (it probably wasn't so soft as all that) at Redcar on his penultimate appearance. By the time he runs on fast ground again, we fancy he'll have come down the handicap the few pounds necessary to resume his winning ways. Another point about The Can Can Man is that he is a hard-pulling type whose dam was a sprinter, and we just wonder whether he'll be better suited to (and therefore show improved form) racing over six furlongs and seven furlongs, rather than the mile over which he was asked to do the bulk of his work as a three-year-old. He has been known to give considerable trouble at the stalls. **M. Johnston**

TIDEMARK (USA) ❙ 4 b.c. Riverman (USA)
Remarkably (USA) (Prince John)

No stranger to success in good-quality handicaps in recent years, Luca Cumani looks to have the right sort of horse to continue his run in the useful Tidemark. Forgive Tidemark his failure to land any part of the huge prize on offer in the Festival Handicap at Ascot in September last time out: he's much better than that but seemed unsuited by the modest gallop. In a really strongly-run affair over the same distance and ground at the Ebor meeting the previous month he'd put up a cracking performance to finish second to the rallying Comstock in the Knavesmire Handicap, pipped on the line after quickening well. That was an improvement of around a stone on any of his previous form, which included wins at Newcastle and Epsom.

The distance at York and Ascot was a mile and a half, the ground good to firm; he has also won over a mile and a quarter on dead. Given a true pace and a fair weight (he starts the season on a lenient mark), Tidemark will make his presence felt in some of the better middle-distance handicaps this term. **L. M. Cumani**

WAKASHAN ❙ 3 b.c. Dancing Brave (USA)
Lady Moon (Mill Reef (USA))

If Wakashan proves anywhere near as good, and we reckon he will, as his Kris half-sister Moon Cactus and half-brother Shining Steel, both also trained by Cecil, he's bound to win a good race or two. From Dancing Brave's first crop, Wakashan will be well suited by middle distances. His dam Lady Moon, a winner three times who gave the impression she would have been well suited by a mile and three quarters or more, is a close relation to Main Reef. In his one race at two—the one-mile Whatcombe Stakes at Newbury in which the likes of Quest For Fame, Deploy and Carroll House have been placed in recent years—Wakashan travelled well racing up with the pace, quickened a couple of lengths clear with Another Bob, who'd already had one run, at the distance, but couldn't quite sustain his challenge to the line. Ryan wasn't hard on him, and Wakashan was beaten two and a half lengths by Another Bob and All The King's Men, the latter of whom went on to win a listed race at Milan next time out. A lengthy, rather angular colt with scope, Wakashan is obviously well regarded—he was heavily supported at Newbury and went off favourite—and he's certain to benefit considerably from his debut. His backers should have ample opportunities to get their money back. **H. R. A. Cecil**

WALIM (USA) | 3 ch.c. Nijinsky (CAN)
 Splendid Girl (USA) (Golden Eagle (FR))

Walim's form was only quite useful at two, but significantly he improved appreciably with each of his four races, and we've almost certainly yet to see the best of him. He gained his sole victory when stepped up to a mile and a quarter in a maiden at Nottingham in October. He did it impressively, too, quickening under pressure early in the straight and being able to coast the closing stages. Walim's performance at Nottingham earned him a run in the Jennings The Bookmakers Zetland Stakes, a listed race over the same trip at Newmarket in November. In the event, he was beaten three quarters of a length by Matahif, the winner of another division of the same Nottingham maiden, but he again showed improved form in finishing second.

Walim is big and rangy, and just the sort to make a better three-year-old. He's well bred, too, being by Nijinsky out of Splendid Girl, a seven-time winner in the States, whose first foal was the top-class French miler Thrill Show (by Northern Baby) who went on to win a division of the Hollywood Derby. David's Bird was another good winner in the States for the dam, but two of Splendid Girl's English-trained runners failed to uphold the family name. Walim, who'll stay at least a mile and a half, could well put things right in 1991, particularly given a wet spring. He acts well on soft ground. **M. R. Stoute**

Walim's sire Nijinsky wins from Blakeney in the mile-and-a-half King George VI and Queen Elizabeth Stakes